T0196216

Sometimes I Think

Poems

ANGELA MARIE

authorHOUSE®

AuthorHouse™
1663 Liberty Drive
Bloomington, IN 47403
www.authorhouse.com
Phone: 1 (800) 839-8640

Published by AuthorHouse 01/16/2017

ISBN: 978-1-5246-5966-0 (sc)
ISBN: 978-1-5246-5965-3 (e)

Print information available on the last page.

About the Author... Angela Marie

Angela Marie is an inspired writer, wife, mother and educator.

She attended Temple University for her undergraduate degree and earned her Master's degree from Grand Canyon University. She is a recipient of the Curtis Thomas Teacher's Award and served as an Educator of young children for over twenty-four years.

Angela is Christian and desires to uplift, encourage, and lead human kind toward a sober and sound emotional state.

Angela enjoys rendering Dramatic-Read-Alouds of her work. Contact her at http://www.poemsbyangelamarie.com/ for an affordable reservation.

See Also: Black White and Mocha Cream Poems and After Sunday Mo'nin' Poems by Angela Marie.

Photo by Kym-Stevens

Table of Contents

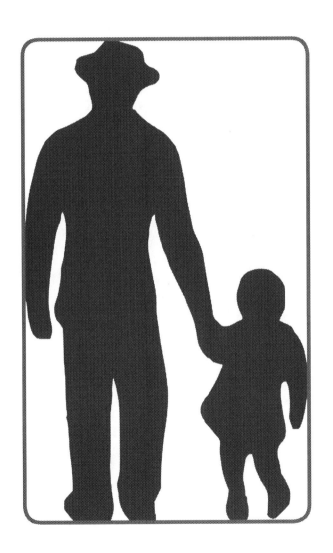

Smooth Backs

by Angela Marie Written July 18th 2015 @ 1:45 p.m.

I looked at my baby born with a back without whelps...
And because we were free I hoped he would never
See or feel the cowhide rip his flesh to yelp...

He ran in the fields...
He picked cotton next to me...

Though free we lived in Slave Quarters...
We were free...

I knew how to read a little...
And I would show him how...

My baby with a smooth back...
I would teach him now...

My baby boy would be a man...
Not a mere boy, jimmy niggah, or less than a dog...
My baby picked cotton next to me...
But my smooth backed baby was free...

We lived in slave quarters but I stood as a Man...
My smooth backed baby...

Would understand the pride of a man and the
Meaning of free...

Though he id the *jim crow dance next to me...
we were free...

I knew how to read a little...
And I would show him how...

My baby with a smooth back...
I would teach him...
I would teach him...
I would teach him...
How to be free...
While I'm still running from a lynching...But...we are free
*the author intentionally used lower case letters to intentionally be little Jim Crow

Worried Mask

by Angela Marie Written July 8, 2015 @9:35 p.m.

I wore a mask
    That extended from my calves to my hairline...
    But I didn't intend to put it on...

My brow scowled
    Though I manicured them...
      And the financial stress...

Turned off utilities and the mortgage paid late...
    And worries about how and what to eat...
      Oozed from within...

        As my thoughts
          Organized and prioritized
            Thoughts about them...

      The worried mask coated my voice
        As my patience grew short...

      I put on my make up and braided my hair...
        But the pressure of my stressor I did wear...
      My hand on my hip, without my knowledge...
        I worked hard at smiling...

That smile,
    A muddled grimace...
I fought my mental instability
    Not to stay in it...

The mask forlorn and glued to my face...
    Oh Lord....
      Keep my waning faith...
       Help me out of this...

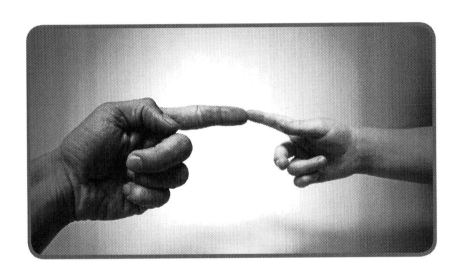

My Dear Josiah...

By Angela Marie

I want the best for you, Chil'...

One day you will be a man...
I want the best for you, Chil'...
Do you understand?
Make the right choices about
your production in school...
Make the right choices in what
you do and don't do...
Your success Chil'....
Depends on you...
Your success Chil'....
Depends on you...
One day you will be a man...
I want the best for you, Chil'...
Do you understand?
Pray to the LORD and read the HOLY, GOD
BREATHED SCRITURES...
For the WORDs of Christ will be your redemption...
I want the best for you, Chil'...
Learn what you can...
Choose good friends...
Do you understand?
Be slooooooowww to anger...
And spread your laughter...
And wise in how you love....
I want the best for you Chil'

I want the best for you, Josiah...

With Love,
Mommy

Dear Josiah,

This poem is dedicated to you. You are maturing into a wonderful young man.
When you were growing inside of me, I loved you. When you were born, I loved you more. I love you. I love you. I love you!

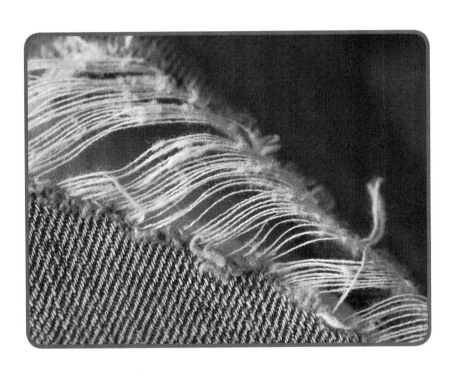

Raggedy Seams

**by Angela Marie Written July 7th 2015 @12:42 a.m.
Revised July 27th 2016 @ 7:47 a.m.**

The girl of 9 wanted to be a Physical Therapist...
She was told she wasn't smart enough to handle it...

Then a prison was built to secure her future...

Then at 10, she decided to be a Lawyer...

She was told that she lacked the natural skills...
And for her the bars for her cell were built...

Then at 11, she decided to be a Sport's Caster...
Again discouraged
and then...

She saw her brown brothers beat down on television...

A seam in her heart was rent...

All of her dreams shattered....
A Lawyer...
A Physical Therapist...
A Sport's Caster...
It didn't matter....

Then at 12 she tried again...
"I want to be a politician!"

Once again she heard discouraging words...
And the raggedy seam grew bigger...
And the absurd...
Started to happen...
She turned 13
And 14
And eventually 26....
And she never did forget any of it...

She lawyered and became a politician...

She manages

She defends
She followed her dream....
But there is a hole in her heart...
A raggedy seam...

Sometimes if you listen as she debates...
You can hear subtle torture and hate...

Though she followed her dream...
Within her heart is a raggedy seam...

It has grown bigger as she matured...
And she is mending it with the LOVE of the LORD...

Still her heart has a raggedy seam...
Sometimes she cries...
Sometimes she screams...
Because the little girl suffered from low self esteem
and
Built prisons for her with a cell intended for her claim...
But Praise the Lord none of that came...

No longer a girl of 9, 10, 11, 12, or 13,
the woman... achieves...
Holding up the little girl with raggedy seams...

Groove

by Angela Marie written July 9, 2015 @10:45 a.m.

I can't do this anymore!!!!!
I can't wear my hair the way
the they
want me to...

I can't do my dance to the tune of
the they tunes
set on my juke....

I can't jump and jive and hide my intellect...
Either way...
The they
Disrespect...

Me...

I can't do this anymore!!!
I can't say yessah nossah...
When I can speak the King's language fo' sho'
I can't do this shufflin' dance anymore...

I can't do **my** dance to the tune of
the they tunes
set on **my** juke...

I can't live **my** whole life to the cadence...
The mind set of another's tune...

Approval
Approval
Is
The bottom line...

I no longer need the sing songy nursery rhyme...
I'm not Cinderella, Snow White, or Mary had a little lamb...

I have to be **me** and groove to **my** own jamm.

Deleted

by Angela Marie Written July 10, 2015 @ 11:49 a.m.

I had to rewind, erase, and delete thoughts about me...
The emotional abuse that gripped me...
Made a deep impression on the crevices of my mind and made a deep impression on the understanding of my heart

All About Me...

I made a mistake...
I dropped a plate....
And immediately my mind went to self hate...

I was stupid because my hand slipped...
I was insane because the tears came...
I had to rewind, erase and delete thoughts about me...
The emotional abuse that gripped me...
Made a deep impression on the crevices of my mind and made a deep impression on the understanding of my heart...

All About me...

I was retarded because I hesitated to respond
To a conversation about deer and fawn...
And immediately my mind...
Went to self hate...

Those words were told to me over and over and over and over and over and over and over And over and over and over and over and over and over and over and over

I believed them after the one-thousandth time.
Then after the words
The hits came.
The words
The slap
The bruise
All the same...

So...

When I did finally escape...
I had to erase the mental tapes
That played without end...

I had to erase those tapes...
Renew my mind as I learned about me.
And learned of God's Pure love toward me.

Time
Time
The gift of Time...
The renewing of my mind...
The learning of God's mercy and grace...
Helped me to erase.
Tapes of Self-hate...

I learned that I like vanilla...
I learned that I like my home neat
I learned that the sound of my own laughter is sweet...

I learned of my intellect
Not dumb at all....

Sometimes the tape plays again...
But now that I'm free...
I choose not to listen...
And not to listen at all...

To My Husband,
I love you dearly. You are a
genuinely good man. I will
always remember your deep
voice and resonating rich cello
tones....
I love you....Angela

Sound of Love

by Angela Marie written July 23, 2016 @ 9:44 p.m.

I was driving and bopping around
And bopping around...
      I used the car speaker to call my husband
            To hear the soothing of his voice
               The oozing of his voice...
As usual at the close of the conversation...
          He said, "I love you"
          And automatically,
          I responded, "I love you too."
          As we always do...As we always do...
He took a deep deep deep pause like never before...
And said with a deliberate tone...
     "No
     IIIIIIII
     loooooove
     yoooooooooou"

I found myself tickled and blushed.....
This was different from the mundane and ordinary rush
         This exchange touched my heart....
      I heard that my husband.... Meant it...
         There was more I heard when he said it....
         He said with a deep pause like never before...
         And said with a deliberate tone...

"IIIIIII
LOOOOOVE
YOOOOOOUUUU" I heard it with my heart...
        Beyond my eardrum....
          I heard with my heart...
          Beyond the normal humdrum...
           And it touched me sooo...
            His words embraced me...
              His words made me pause...
             To listen to His love...
               And I heard him...
               And
               I
               Heard
               Him...

Escaped Tilt

by Angela Marie Written July 10, 2015 @ 9:46 a.m.

I was rescued from a pit...
I was rescued from out of it...

I was liking where I was...
I was liking what I was doing...
Like the beginning of taking drugs...
It consumes you

I was rescued from a pit...
I was rescued from out of it...

I was laughing and playing along...
Until I learned that my actions were wrong...

The problem with that knowledge is that it seemed too late...
The drug like think took me over...
A Destined Fate?

I kept inhaling the incense tilted toward my incline...
I had to get out. And stop it...
To save my life....

I was rescued from a pit...
I was rescued from out of it...

I was liking where I was...
I was liking what I was doing...
Like the beginning of taking drugs...
It consumes you....

So...somebody prayed for me...
Had me on their mind....

And Jesus stepped in on time...

It would be a fairytale
if I told you that it happened just like that...
Yes, it was a grueling, a grueling, and freeing process...
A freeing process...

Somebody prayed for me...
Had me on their mind....
And called on Jesus....
And I escaped to save my life...
That tilt...
That incline...

A freeing process still....
I fight not be re-entangled in the will of the ill...

Shirley Ruth Says

by Angela Marie
Written Friday, July 8, 2016 @ 7:28 p.m.

Shirley Ruth says with tones of

lemon meringue pie

      and the nutrients

          of collard greens...

'Pray, Pray, Pray...

      Pray like you breathe...

          often...'

Shirley Ruth says with a spoonful

of sweet potato pie

      and a scoop of

          baked macaroni

          and cheese...

'Minister when you sing...

      do not perform...

          Minister and sing

          Unto the LORD...'

Shirley Ruth says with aromas

      of sugar, flour, milk,

          butter and eggs

          whipped into a batter...

'A relationship with Jesus gives you depth, protection, and eternal life...'

Shirley Ruth says with savory memories of fried chicken,

      candied yams, and buttered

      cornbread

          hanging off of the plate...

Love each other and your

          love vat

          will never grow empty...'

Shirley Ruth says with the hues and resonance of a melodic soprano...
'Jesus is bigger than the giants you encounter...

Dedicated to Mommy...

Anyone that has sat with you for a few minutes or more...

Has gained applicable knowledge and wisdom...

With Love,
Angela

Jesus is bigger than the booming voice you hear...'

Shirley Ruth says with a sip of
            iced water
                    and a hint of pecan pie...

'Respect the position
            if you can't respect
            the person in the position...'

Shirley Ruth says with the
warmth of her heart
            and the icing of a cupcake...

"I LOVE YOU."

'Accept Jesus in your heart as LORD and Savior....

Repent and live a consecrated life unto HIM.'

"I LOVE YOU."

Just To Be There
by Angela Marie Written7/6/2015 @ 10:43 a.m.

Beyond the Blueness of the sky...
So Close to the Glory of God's eye...

To lay at the feet of Jesus
And weep...

Just to be there...

To sing to Who Christ IS...
To sing to HIS LORD of LORDSHIP!!

To breathe in HIS presence!
To breathe in THE essence
Of
GOD!

To see the bluest of blue
And the goldest of gold...
To sit in view of JESUS on the THRONE...
Just to be there...
In God's vastness
In God's Presence...
To breathe HIS ESSENCE...
Just to be there...

Memories With a Kiss

by Angela Marie written 10/4/2014 @ 9:16 a.m.

I remember

    Her how are you doings

        And how are you doings candor...

           And depth of concern

               For me and my soul...

Dedicated to the memory of my neighbor and former babysitter....

I remember her voice from

As

Young

As

Two

Years

Old...

I'll remember her laughter

    And

      What are we going to do about **that?**

    I mean only me and she knew about the **that!**

    I'll remember...

    Her How are you doings

    And

    How are you doings candor

    And the depth of concern

    For me and my soul...

        I remember her voice and laughter

        From as young as

        Two

        Years Old...

        I will miss her...

        Yes... I will remember with a smile and pleasant grin...

Because the depth of her soul...

    Resides in heaven... These are my memories with a kiss

Precious Baby

by Angela Marie Written July 10, 2015 @ 9:23 a.m.
(Early Memories of my son)

Oh how precious he was....
He looked into my eyes with love...

Oh how precious he was...
He drank from my breast to live...

Oh how precious he was....
To nestle close to me...

Oh how precious he was...
My precious baby...

His cry sweet, like the scent of cornbread...
I smiled at the tenderness of how he turned his little head...

His laughter, like an easy giggle box...
I love this little boy more than a lot...

Oh how precious he is...
I look at him with love...

Oh how precious he is...
My son...

My Friend died
by Angela Marie Written July 7, 2015 @ 9:44 a.m.

I miss how she spoke with so much glee...
> I miss her tremendously...

I'm really upset and mad about it...
cancer stole her life...
The medicine...the struggle... added so much strife...

I think about her children...
Her offspring...
And how they must miss their only mommy.

I miss her tremendously...
I miss how she spoke with so much glee...

I'm really upset and mad about it...
Cancer took her life...
The medicine...the struggle... added so much strife...

My body shook with grief...
I held my head in disbelief...

Oh, how I miss her...

One thing for sure...
Her eternity is secure...
She accepted Jesus in her heart...
Just before her delicate depart...

I miss her tremendously...
I'm really upset and mad about it...
Cancer stole her life...

I haven't wholly come to terms with it...
Only one thing
Helps me cope
With it...

She made her peace with Christ...
She secured her eternal life...

Haven't wholly come to terms with it...
Only one thing
Helps me cope
With it...

She made her peace with Christ...
She secured her eternal life...
She secured her eternal life...
I need to do the same....

Familial Trend

by Angela Marie Written July 8, 2015@ 10:03 p.m.

Your bloodline is deeper than the lilt of your brow and the way you kick out your foot and the duplication of your looks...

Some of it is your behavior
      The thought processes you present...
                  It's in your cadence of speech...
                  Its deep...

Some of your duplication is from your environment...
      Its what you breathed from mommy and daddy that touches your natural bend...
                  Some behaviors are familial trends...

Some of your duplication goes back where you can't see...
Pay attention to the good, the bad, the beauty, the ugly...

            There is a bloodline that transcends all...
IT covers...
IT cleanses...
      familial ick....
            bloodline sins...
                  Our sinful nature that resides within...

                  The Blood of Jesus is what I mean...
                        Accept Jesus and be made clean...

Do understand that your family may have gifts....
      But give it to Jesus...
            The GIVER of the gift...
                  And the ills and ick that exists...
                  Why not be the first to stop it.

Orchestrated Presence

Written July 8, 2015 @ 2:13 p.m.

There I lay
> On my hospital bed...
>> My strength and breath waning...
> and I said, "Please don't let me die?"

Soon after,
> I was asleep, not aware...
>> ...my presence of mind absent...
>>> But Jesus was there...

The Lord orchestrated the nurse's presence...
> or I would have been dead that day...

They gave me some medicine that startled me to wake...

And I give THE FATHER, SON, & HOLY SPIRIT
> my Praise!!!!
> I am so relieved that THE LORD intervened...
>> Interceded for me...
>>> Jesus is LORD...
>>>> The KING of kings...
>>>>> To GOD BE THE GLORY

Cane

by Angela Marie written July 9, 2015@ 12:39 p.m.

Now when I see a cane...
I see the associated pain...
I see past the grieving look on your face...

I see the bone spurs
I see the bones pounding at every physical turn...

I hear the sadness because your speed doesn't match the movement in your mind...

I hear the clickety clack of your bones hitting your responsive nerves...

Sitting
Standing
Walking
Standing still...

I see how your lack of movement has affected your weight...
But with every move...
There is an iron weighted gate...

To push...

I hear the clickety clack of your bones hitting your responsive nerves...
I see the bone spurs...

I hear the cry behind your retina...
I hear your screams and the pain that eats ya...

Take my hand...
Let me drive...
Let me try to assist you...

Between walking and pain...
Joy and an expressed jog...

Is the cane...
And the associated pain...

Let me help ya.

Don't Drink the Poison

By Angela Marie Written July 10, 2015 @ 9:10 a.m.

Don't drink the poison...
Whether it be words or a drug...
Don't imbibe the venomous wine into your emotional, spiritual,
or physical vein...
For trust that it will kill you if you drink...

Don't drink the poison
Whether it be ostracized attitude or abusive cling...
Those poisons do the same thing...

They suffocate
And cause you to hold your head low...
And breathe with a frailty...
One should never never know...

Don't' drink the poison
Whether it be served from familial hands or not...
Don't drink the poison...
Death is the intended plot...

Don't' drink the poison
Even if served with a smile

Behind that smile is guile and a blooded knife waiting to be stabbed again
into your back...
So... don't drink the poison whether served by family, friend, or foe...

Don't drink the poison...
Avoid...
Rid yourself of that subtle woe!!!!

Don't drink the poison...
Drink healthful things...
Don't drink the poison...
Don't make your tragedy their gain...

Don't drink the poison...
Not anymore...
Grow and Grow...
And be fruitful and mature....

Don't drink the poison...

Gawk

by Angela Marie Written July 11, 2015 @ 3:41 p.m

There were eyes
Just eyes
Staring at me...
I was startled and screaming
The eyes kept gawking at me...
I was standing in the middle of the street...
though a throng around me...
The eyes kept looking at me...

Some of the eyes began to speak...
Against my ambitions...
Against my zeal...
Against the feelings that I feel...

They spoke against any self-proclamation...
Or point of pride I may have gained....
The eyes were shouting...
Negative words
Again and again...

How do you not to listen
when the words came from people close to you...
I have learned to decipher what is real and untrue...
And when you get tired of being gawked at...
you get tired of the eyes...
people gawking, staring...
analyzing you down to
the hair follicle to the left of your nose....
What do you do...

I prayed...
I prayed against the clamor that came at my inside...
I invited Jesus to help me through my plight...
I cried...
I prayed...
I cried...

I prayed....
And HE sent people that liked me...
HE sent people that loved all of me...
HE sent friends, family.....

        HE helped me to be able to stand alone...
        To be all of successful in all of my layers...
        Multiple zones....

        I'm standing...

Insult

by Angela Marie Written 7/6/2015 @ 1:45 p.m.

OOOh Chile...
He was fine to me!
He was cultured and the tone of his voice was melodic...
You see!

> But...
> When I tell you what I'm about to say...
> I was totally surprised...
> That fine man was gay!

> > Maybe he wasn't...
> > But he had to be...
> > I enticed him
> > And invited him...
> > To be with me...
> > Sexually...

> > > As fine as I am...
> > > How could he resist!
> > > To lay down with me...
> > > A fine enchantress...

> That man...
> Who had to be gay...
> Told me he wanted to wait 'til marriage...
> And not play...

Ooh Chile...
How could he deny me...
A fine drink of joy...
He insulted me...

Something was wrong with him...
To deny a feline like this...
A fine, beautiful, curvaceous, goddess...Mmmh.

In Reply

by Angela Marie Written 7/6/2015 @ 9:59 a.m.(in response to the poem, Insult)

She was fine...
And beautiful to see...
But I had to stand
Or run
For my integrity...

I heard of a story...
    Joseph was his name...
    And he ran when a beautiful woman
    Did the same...

        So, Enchantress smeared my name with dung...
        But I know in the depths of my loins...
        She won't birth
            Or regurgitate
                To feed my young...

          I chose to marry another...
            To bare my name...
               So your accusations are shameless
                 And vain...

               There is so much more to you
               Than your hair...
               Your eyes...
               Your figure...
               Your physical design...

There is more to you Enchantress...
I wanted to engage your mind...
    For your mind enhances your physical design
    And the governing of your soul as well...

You need...   I need...   We all need...
To pull ourselves out of the pit of STD Spreading Hell...
Think About it...

No More Share Croppin'

by Angela Marie written July 16, 2015 @ 7:33 p.m.

No shoes on ma feet...
Ice and snow on the wet soil... the earth...

Stood behind the mule...
And put my hands to the plow...

Ice and snow on the wet soil...the earth...
No shoes on ma feet....
Ice and rain and snow on the wet soil...the earth...
No shoes on ma feet...

The mule plopped and urinated as he plodded along...
I stood in it...
To warm ma feet...
I stood in it...
To warm ma feet...

That dung and urine
Was warmth to me...

That's only a moment of my share croppin' story...

I plodded along in overalls....
In the rain...
In the snow...
No shoes on ma feet...
The mule and I plodded along...
Didn't feel like singin' no kinda song....

Stood behind the mule...
And put my hands to the plow...

Ice and snow on the wet soil... the earth...
No shoes on ma feet...

I had to do it....
And a Jim Crow Dance...
In order to eat...

Buster

And I Wept Blue Tears

by Angela Marie written 7/24/2016 @ 9:20 p.m.

And I wept blue tears...
Indigo even...
And I wept blue tears...
Without a reason...

Then I wept blue and black tears
And I couldn't stop...

I wept tears of bruisings
Without a cause...

And I slept relentlessly
But, the fatigue never left...
And I wept blue tears
And black tears
And I wept and wept...

I slouched
And I grimaced, an attempt at a smile...
But I wept...
And I wept...
And I wept for a while...
Undone hair and mismatched socks...
I cried and slept and the fatigue never left...

I couldn't control it...
I couldn't pray it away...
My emotions...
Broken...
Like a broken leg...

The doctor with a sunbathed tan and Italian Shoes...
Wrote on a pad and told me what to do...

The chemistry in my brain was off balance and wrong...
My brain...
Hormones of blue and varying hues...

Chemicals and chemistry rising and falling off cue!

Wisdom this time in the medicine prescribed...
Gave my body the balance it naturally deprived...

The medicine helped lift emotional decay...
But even with the medicine....
I need to pray!
God gave wisdom and knowledge about plants...
So...there was a remedy...
An emotional cast...

No longer walking around sad and forlorn....
I'm able to trust in the provisions of the LORD....

The medicine helped correct the emotional decay...
Just like diabetes or a broken or crushed leg...

Naked To See Me...

by Angela Marie written 7/25/2016 @ 10:55 a.m.

I made up my face...
Foundation
Lipstick
Lashes
Liner
And all...

Though all made up...
I didn't feel pretty at all...

Designer labels...
Heels and matching bag...
I bought all this stuff
But there is something I don't have...

Perfumed all over in my favorite scent...
Still there is something missing in all that I've spent...

Men glancing with rays of merriment...
But none drawing close enough for a lifelong commitment...

When I look at me
I am indeed an educated catch...
But it seems that there is something that I can't quite get...

I am a diva
And I know I am fine...
Perhaps men are intimidated by this feline...
Perhaps their confidence is deflated...
Perhaps they are threatened by the awesome of me...
What is it that makes them flee from me....
Why is it that I can't please them
And they can't please me...

I see other women
Plain as a bucket or pail...
And they have men that love them...
And love them off the rails!

In my mind I am every man's desire...
At least that's what I portray in my outward attire...

So...
When I go home...
And shed my outer skin...
All that is left are lashes in the trash and designer labels in the wash...
And I have to embrace and deal with my inner self...

So I examine as my height is shortened because I kicked off those heels...
And as I began to pray...
God showed me for real...

I have some issues...
Some small...
Some tall...
Some kinda rank...

And I saw that as I dressed my inside stank...

I never dressed my spirit...
I never dressed the heart of my mind...
I never washed my conscious with soft tones to speak kind...

Never put a shoe
To step into humbleness...

Never put on a lash
To soften another's pain...

And If I did those things...
It was my invisible pin of honor to gain...

I never dressed my spirit
In all of that dressing...

I never dressed my heart
In all of the awesome of me...

I had to be quiet and naked for me to see...
To see
Me.

It Is Good!

By Angela Marie written February 9th 2016 @7:54 p.m.

Dedicated to a
Chef and friend!

That gal over there,
Made some Sweet Potato Cheesecake and my lips sang...
It Is Good!
Joy leaped into my belly as the ingredients sank beneath my
Taste buds
And my lips sang...
It
Is
Good!

Laughter and smiles danced on my fork
As I swallowed with glee...
And my lips sang again
It
Is
Good!

And
It was...
It was...
For real...
And I ate it all...

A Game of Disdain
by Angela Marie Written 7/25/2016 @ 12:15 p.m.

They look at me as I walk to the drug house...
They look at me trying to figure me out...
And I walk with a need in my strut...
And I walk because I need that stuff...

I walk up the steps and knock on the door...
I walk up the steps to needle the cure ...

They look at me not able to help...
They look at me not wanting to either...
They look at me reprimanding my fever...

I feel the sickness...
I feel the withdrawal...
I need my medicine...
Regardless of their scowls...
I need my medicine whatever way I can get it...
I need my medicine and I'm going to get it...

They look at me making a judgment...
They look at me not knowing that I don't want to want it...

They look at me as I sell myself...
But they don't know that their husbands and wives help me to sell it
        because they are my buyers and I don't even have to dance...
        I just offer myself and they jump at the chance....

They are takers in this game of disdain...

I need my medicine whatever way I can get it...
I need my medicine and I'm going to get it...

I didn't know that the lady that stared...
Saw herself and for me she was scared...

She saw me...
She was me...
And in all that my need entails...

And she prayed and cried
and for me
She Wailed....

I thought she was scowling...
Like most of them do...

She was interceding...
She knew how to...

I didn't know that
that lady cared in her stares...
I didn't know that for me and herself...
She was scared...

She watched me stop and start the game of disdain again and again...
She understood the rut, the state of mind I was in...

I looked at her with disdain not knowing that for me she prayed...
Perhaps one day from my need...
I'll stay away...

Your It Thing
by Angela Marie Written 2/8/2016 @6:57 a.m.

You are somebody
And
Your words are important...
And
Don't stand in the corner cowering
Your
Words
Your
Stance
Your
You
Can
Be empowering
Just
Speak...
Just go...
Just speak...
Just grow...
Just
Do
The
It thing...
Just walk in who you are without shame or apology...
Just do the
It thing...
And
I
Mean...
Whatever your
It...
Might be...
Teaching...
Speaking...
Consoling a friend...
Just stand in your stance and be free...
And be
Who God made you to be...
Just
Do your
It
Thing...

Quenched
by Angela Marie written 7/25/2016 @ 1:55 p.m.

I am the woman at the well...
I drank water from cisterns that were not my own...
I am the woman at the well and I drink again and again
from the cisterns of multiple men and my soul is parched....

I am the whore where army men come and await my service...
I am the woman that men tell their secrets to
And I caress them and they trust me
And my soul is parched in and out of their company...

I am the woman that bleeds...
I am the woman that seeks...
I am the woman that gets kicked to the side when I cry tears of olive oil...
I am the woman you seek after...
And my soul is parched...
My throat is dry...
My heart is peeling....

I am the woman at the well...
I am the whore that men tell their secrets to...

I am the woman who veils her true depth and identity,

Yet CRIMSON covers me...
Yet CRIMSON from the right hand of God rescued
a dying
emaciated
peeling
decrepit
soul...
me....

From a Boy

by Angela Marie

Dear Teacher,

My name is boy.
I want to learn,
Just don't redirect me...
Just teach me as I am...

Young and vulnerable...

I'm hurting
I'm in pain
Mommy took that glass pipe and inhaled...
Mommy nodded, nodded, nodded...
And I cried for milk...

Mommy nodded, nodded, nodded...

I want to learn
Just don't redirect me...
Just teach me as I am...

Young and Vulnerable...

I'm angry
But I don't know that I am...
Don't know what I am...
Don't know who I am...

Just teach me as I am...

Young and vulnerable...

Mommy nodded, nodded, nodded...

I'm hurting
I'm in pain
But I don't know that I am...
Don't know what I am...
Don't know who I am...

I cried for milk...

Mommy nodded, nodded, nodded...

I want to learn...
Just teach me as I am...

I flop tables
And I cuss in your face...
I reach down in my pant and masturbate...

I cuss and fight anyone that looks like me
Bigger than me
Smaller than me

Anyone that appears to bother me
Real or imagined...

I want to learn...
Really I do...

Just teach me as I am...

Young Vulnerable...

I'm angry
But I don't know that I am...
Don't know what I am...
Don't know who I am...

Just teach me how to read.
Just teach me how to count.
Just teach me how to speak...

I'm sorry for flipping the tables...
I'm sorry for punching the teachers and students in the face...

Just teach me...
As I am...

Young and Vulnerable...

I'm angry
I'm hurting

Will the system nod on me too...
Will the teacher nod on me too?

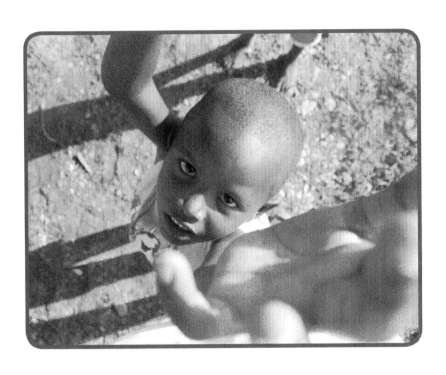

Reach

a message from one child, to the hearts of many that teach
written by Angela Marie June 30, 2015 @8:46 a.m.

Reach inside the hearts and minds
of us...

Scaffold us upward...

To the places we need to be...

Use the data...
Use our interests...
Use what you see...

Reach to reach the many...
Take my hand and reach me...

Reach

Reach in the archives of your resources...
So that Dick and Jane and Angela and James can read and write and
calculate and problem solve...

Help us to resolve...
Our problems...

Not just to pass the test...
Not just to earn distinguished on your assessment...

But reach...

Reach inside the hearts and minds
of us...

Scaffold us upward...

To the places we need to be...

Take my hand and reach me...

Swinging Vines

by Angela Marie Written 7/26/2016 @ 1:11 p.m.

I am the queen
I am the queen of the region...
The king is my husband...

I am the queen
Not a perfumed concubine...

I am the queen
And yet...

I must *sackcloth my heritage...
I must sackcloth my lineage...
I must sackcloth my ethnicity...
I must sackcloth my me...
I must hide for my own safety...

I am the queen...

Though beautiful and royal and selected by the king...

I must sackcloth my heritage...
I must sackcloth my lineage...
I must sackcloth my ethnicity...
I must sackcloth my me...
I must hide for my own safety...

I am the queen...

I with wisdom and the king's favor...
Enter the court with requests to unveil...

Risking my own existence and life...
As my secret is revealed...

In many situations...
I see myself encountering this plot...

I hide my richness...
I silence my strength...
I suffocate my essence...

To please the king...

And when the moment is right...
The ashes and sackcloth come off...

The same ashes and sackcloth soiled by a retarded time...

The blackened history of me
Saves a people and myself from swinging on tree vines...

The same sackcloth soiled by a retarded time...

Finally unveiled ...
Saves a people and myself from swinging and burning on tree vines...

The king...
My husband....
Put out the command...
To hang that Haman by his own hand...

I am the queen...
And they don't know it...

I am the queen
My influence....
They don't know it...

Be mindful how you treat me...
And those connected to my bloodline...

For if you continue trying to kill me...
You might swing from your own vine...

*Sackcloth: (noun) a garment worn to symbolize sadness, grief, protest, or mourning. Often worn with black ashes placed on the head.

The author took creative license used sackcloth as a verb.

*Haman: Antagonist in the Book of Esther that plotted to kill the Jewish people.

Always at a Deficit...

by Angela Marie written July 26, 2016 @ 6:01 p.m.

Broken pencils
A broken system
And bulging jails...

Why set up the urban school to fail?

Broken pencils
A broken system
Peeling walls
And bulging jails...

Why set up urban schools to fail?

We use obsolete tools
Rusted in plethora...
Obsolete tools rusted in plethora
In plethora...

The urban student is always trying to catch up...
trying to catch up...

He competes in an environment that puts monies in jail...
The infrastructure is designed to fail...

Excited about the use of pre-owned or vintage computers...
While the prisons have new ones for the newly recruited...

Broken pencils
A broken system
The bulging of jails...

Why set up the urban school to fail...
Broken pencils
A broken system
Peeling walls
And bulging jails...
Why set up urban schools to fail?

Crowded classrooms

Though studies have proven the opposite should be done...
But for the urban student the ratio is thirty to one...(30:1)

Leaking ceilings with a bucket to catch the rain...
While students ignore raindrops to train their brains...

Broken pencils
A broken system
The bulging of jails...

Why set up the urban school to fail...
Broken pencils
A broken system
Peeling walls
And bulging jails...
Why set up urban schools to fail...

Sitting in environments with peeling and leaking walls...
Does anyone care about the urban student at all...

Broken pencils
A broken system
And bulging jails...

But somehow many succeed and Learning yet prevails....

From A Teacher...

By Angela Marie written July 27, 2016 @1:04 a. m.

Though the peeling walls in our schools are a distraction...
You and I will make an academic, emotional, and cerebral connection...

Though the combination of music and art is no longer funded...
Because someone found it unnecessary and redundant...

Though your friend died a violent, unfortunate, and early death...
And long-term grief counseling is not available yet...

Though the peeling walls are a distraction...
You and I will make an academic, emotional, and cerebral connection...

And though...
The technology doesn't work
Because of a tiny quirk...

Though there are too many students in the room
And classroom assistants have been removed...

Though the combination of music and art is no longer funded...
Because someone found it unnecessary and redundant...

Though your friend died a violent, unfortunate, and early death...
And long-term grief counseling is not available yet...

Though the peeling walls and leaking ceilings are a distraction...
You and I will make an academic, emotional, and cerebral connection...

Unclung

by Angela Marie written 7/27/2016 @ 1:03 a.m.

I was fourteen and going through fourteen year old changes...
My fourteen-year-old life was rearranging...

Didn't want to be around Grandmommy as much...
I was leaning toward my own stuff...

And it seemed in my fourteen-year-old mind...
That soon after my pulling...
Grandmommy died...

That piece of self-blame...
Stayed with me as I grew...

And I think that is why I cling to you and you and you and you and you...
In my adolescent stunted emotion
It was my way of quieting that confused commotion...

Inept at letting go when I see that it is time...
And...
By clinging...
I was hurt every time....

As I realize the reason for my cling...
I realize that I am maturrrrrriiiiiiiiinnnnnnggggg.

I wasn't the reason why Grandmommy died...
Though I wish with her I had more time...

I hushed the commotion
The cause of my familiar upset...
And early one morn'
Emotion and Commotion met....

I then uncloaked
And vomited the lie that I chose to keep and tell myself
I allowed me to be fourteen in all of its wealth...
And free myself from the lie and blame that no one gave to me...

I gave myself permission to unblame me...

So that I
at 50
and
14
can
be
totally
free...

Clinging
I choose to undo...
Clinging
I choose not to do...
I clung
because of fear of an untruth...

Now I can love without clinging and clinging and clinging to you and you...
Unclung from a teenager's untruth...

Memories of Cotton

by Angela Marie written July 27th, 2016 @ 8:46 a.m.

We went driving Down South...
And I didn't consider the words that escaped my mouth...

I saw beautiful beautiful cotton...
And I said....
"Beautiful beautiful Cotton....
Like Clouds on a stick. Oh I just want to touch it! Press it on my face
and smell it reeeeaaaal close!"
Then I glanced over at Great Great Aunt Rose...
She was crying...
Then I looked at her hands...
She had scars,
that I never ever had....

Then I noticed she was covering her nose...
Great Great Aunt Rose smelled something
Of which I was never exposed...

I didn't smell a thing...
But Great Great Aunt Rose uttered,
"They made my brother swing! Swing! Can't you smell him burning?!"

I looked again at Great Great Aunt Rose...
I saw the old woman crying...
Her hands had scars,
I never ever had...
Her memories of Uncle Booga
His death vulgar and sad...
To the point that the mention of cotton...
Brought back a blackness that she seemingly forgotten...

I looked again
And she started screaming...
What in the world was she remembering?

She began to yell
"Run to the fields! They coming! They coming! They will kill you for real!"

Great Great Aunt Rose had panic in
her eyes...
I couldn't imagine her life...
She started yelling and sobbing about whippings!
She started yelling and sobbing about lies about our History...

She told me, "They will take your tongue out and wear around their necks!"
She had such a fear in her voice, eyes, and body language...
I didn't know what else to expect...

She started to sob some more...
She said, "He raped me and called ME a whore! Then he beat me because
I cried! I was only 9!"

I looked at Aunt Rose through a different lens!
She was always quiet and timid...

Those rows of cotton brought back a lifetime of memory...
And I looked at that cotton again...
It's beauty fading...

In minutes Aunt Rose stopped talking and got quiet again...
She folded her hands and closed her eyes...
She wiped her face...
And stopped her cry...

We went driving Down South
And I listened to Great Great Aunt Rose's quiet...
While I interpreted the history of the South's climate...

And when we got home up North...
I gave Great Great Aunt Rose extra support...
The trauma that woman went through...
Animals had better treatment in zoos.

Get it
by Angela Marie written 7/29/2016 @ 9:18 p.m

On your way to a new beginning
Perhaps shaking in your glittery shoes
But one thing for sure...

Dedicated to those
embarking on a
college degree.

You are going to be alright!
And I know it
And your Momma knows it
And your Daddy knows it...
And your brother knows it...
And we all know it...

You are prepared...
You have the intellect...
You can handle the work
Though you don't know what to expect!

On your way to a new beginning...
Perhaps shaking in your Nikes or Jordan's
But one thing for sure...

You are going to be alright!
And your Momma knows it
And your Daddy knows it...
And your brother knows it...
And we all know it...

I want you to know it too...
You are prepared for whatever task they ask of you...

I am soooo proud of you!
I'm speaking to you!

And you have a multitude of support
A phone call, a thought, or text away...

And one thing for sure...
You will be juuuusssstt fine...
You will be jusssssttt fine....

You have folks prayin' for you on this not so far away campus....
You   will   be   just   fine...
Chil' ain't nothin' wrong with your mind....

You   will   be   just   fine...

Chil' ain't nothin' wrong with your mind....

Get your education
And Earn it you will!
Get it!

Rebellious Gray

by Angela Marie

I was falling in love with the curly and ethnic texture of my hair...
Finally at the monumental age of 50...

And it curled and volumized...
And it was ethnic...
Afrocentric to my eyes...
And then I stopped...

And looked...

And it didn't curl...
It stood straight up in the air...
The rebellious gray and perfectly straight hair...
It wouldn't go up!
It wouldn't go down!
It wouldn't lay to the side...

Just straight up in the air...
That stupid straight hair wouldn't move anywhere!

And I was loving my hair...
Its curl
Its sheen
Its volumized look and ethnic personality...
Finally at the monumental age of 50...

And it wouldn't go up
It wouldn't go down
It just stood there

Straight up in the air!
Straight up there!

Can you see it?

I saw it all day!

And the gray hair yelled out "HEY EVERYBODY!"
And my kindergarten students saw it and pushed it and it popped up again!

Stupid Gray hair was in rebellion!
Rebellion to the curl...
Rebellion to my afro centric hair world...
Just straight up and doing its own thing!
Lie a crooked chicken wing...
mmm

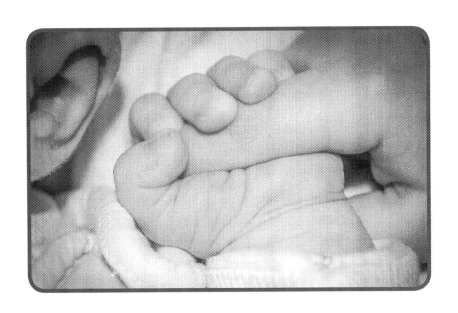

Josiah's Song

by Angela Marie

Josiah Josiah
You are my little boy.
Josiah Josiah
You bring me so much joy.
Josiah Josiah
You are a gift to me!
Josiah Josiah
Jesus with him be!
I love you
I love you
I love you love you love you!
I love you
I love you
I love you love you love you!
I love you
I love you
I love you love you love you!
I love you
I love you
I love you love you love you!

I sung this to and with my son Josiah, when he was a baby.

My Baby

by Angela Marie written July 29ᵗʰ, 2016 @ 9:53 a.m.

I didn't' know about so much love...
There was an outpour of love cascading from me to him...
I never ever experienced this before...

And then our eyes met...
His eyes fastened on mine...
I was in awe and afraid for the very first time...

I prayed...
Oh God this is an AWESOME task...
To raise this child....
This little boy...
Please help me...
This task is too big...
Help Me! Help Me!
And HE did
And is...

The baby needed help to hold his little head...
EVERYTHING he needed he needed from me...
The AWESOME responsibility frightened me
As I held him in my lap and arms...

Though very much engulfed in that moment of oozing love and its comfort...

I was afraid at the same time...

So I prayed for provisions throughout his lifetime...
I loved him...
I love him...
I really really do...
And I never knew a mother's love before that...

Not before I gave birth...
A precious moment,
I'll never forget...

When I held my baby for the very first time...
My heart holds him just like that...
Even when he is a man of fifty...
He will always be my baby...
My heart holds him just like that...
And I must understand his developmental changes...
Though he will always...
Be my baby...

Exfoliate Me

by Angela Marie written ///10/2016 @ 7:24 p.m.

I saw my face
In the mirror...
My mouth was open...
Because I was speaking...

I saw a powerful woman...
Confident...
I looked again...
I saw my mouth like that of a trout...
A mouth fit for swallowing terrestrial insects, worms, and leeches...

I saw my strength as fragile as tissue paper...
And I saw hidden
Rancid
Bruises that make up, foundation, and exfoliation could not cover or rid...

My innards naked...
Broached...

My mouth...
A growing sepulcher in need of forgiveness...

Jesus help me...
I am sinning in my own self righteousness...
And
I am wearing my righteousness as a waving flag slapping itself for applause...

Jesus exfoliate me...
Wash me clean...
Embrace me...
See my Rancid attitude
and bathe me beautiful.

Printed in the United States
By Bookmasters